Level A Book

Dr. Funster's THINK-A-MINUTES

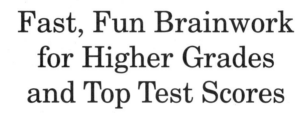

Fast, Fun Brainwork
for Higher Grades
and Top Test Scores

Titles in the series:
Dr. Funster's Think-A-Minutes

Level A Book 1
Level A Book 2
Level B Book 1
Level B Book 2
Level C Book 1
Level C Book 2

© 2002
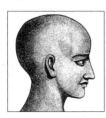
CRITICAL THINKING BOOKS & SOFTWARE
www.criticalthinking.com
P.O. Box 448 • Pacific Grove • CA 93950-0448
Phone 800-458-4849
ISBN 0-89455-806-4
Printed in the United States of America

About Dr. Funster's Think-A-Minutes

This collection of fast, fun riddles, puzzles, and teasers develops thinking skills for higher grades and top test scores. The activities are perfect for school, home, and travel. They are very popular as brain-start, extra credit, sponge, or reward activities.

This collection is taken from a variety of past and current books published by Critical Thinking Books & Software. If you would like to see more of a particular type of activity, refer to page 45 for other pages with similar activities in this book or for the names of the series from which the activities were taken.

For other books with similar activities, call 800-458-4849 for the store nearest you or to order directly.

Which Way?

DIRECTIONS: In how many ways can you get from your house to your friend's house? (Use the diagram below, and follow the arrows.)

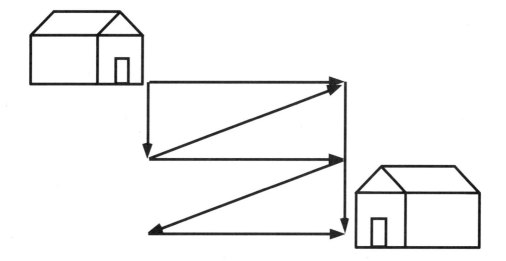

Pass the Fruit, Please

1. Celeste had an apple, a pear, and a banana. She put them in a row. She put the apple to the right of the pear. She put the banana to the right of the apple. Name the way she set the fruits from left to right.

2. Amos had a grape, a lemon, and a watermelon. He put them in a row. He put the largest one in the middle. He put the smallest one to the right of the largest one. Name the way he set the fruits from left to right.

Number Puzzlers

1.   The twins' ages total 22. How old will each be next year?

2.   What number completes this puzzle?

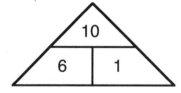 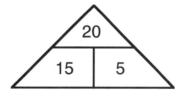 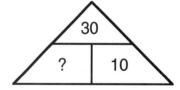

Triangles

How many triangles can you find in this figure?

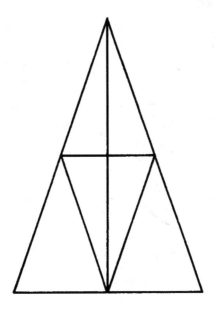

What is True of Both Words?

DIRECTIONS: Decide what the following pairs of words have in common. Circle the letter or letters of the characteristics that are true of both items. These may be more than one answer for each.

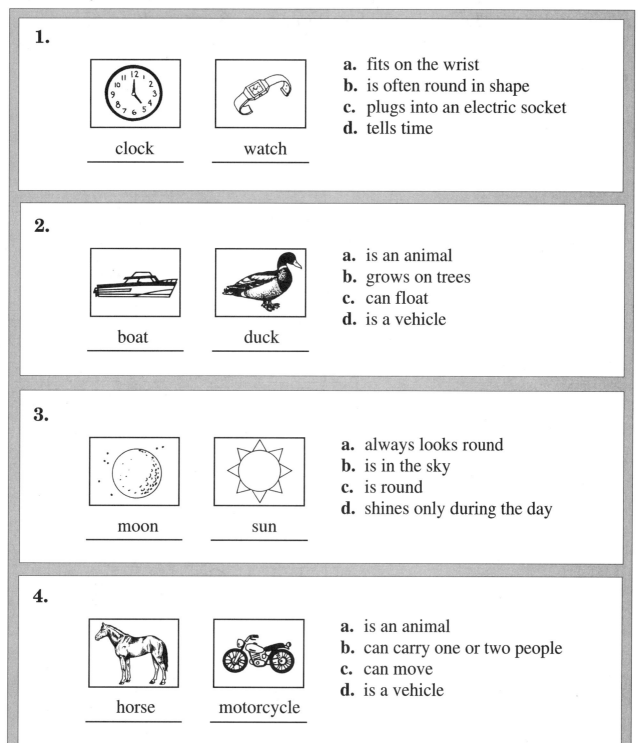

1.

clock   watch

  a. fits on the wrist
  b. is often round in shape
  c. plugs into an electric socket
  d. tells time

2.

boat   duck

  a. is an animal
  b. grows on trees
  c. can float
  d. is a vehicle

3.

moon   sun

  a. always looks round
  b. is in the sky
  c. is round
  d. shines only during the day

4.

horse   motorcycle

  a. is an animal
  b. can carry one or two people
  c. can move
  d. is a vehicle

Mystery Blocks

DIRECTIONS: The blocks in the box are circles, squares, triangles, or rectangles. They are either big or small. They are colored red, yellow, or blue. Use the clues to find the mystery block. Cross out the blocks that do not fit each clue. The blocks can be colored first. B = Blue, R = Red, Y = Yellow.

1.

It is not yellow.

It is small.

It is not a circle.

It has four sides.

It is not a square.

It is red.

It is the

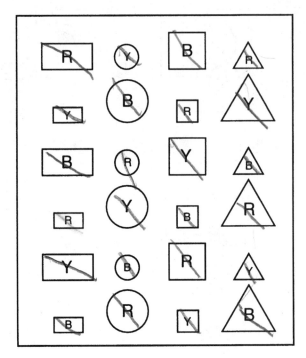

2.

It is not a square.

It is not blue.

It is yellow.

It is not small.

It is not a circle.

It has three sides.

It is the

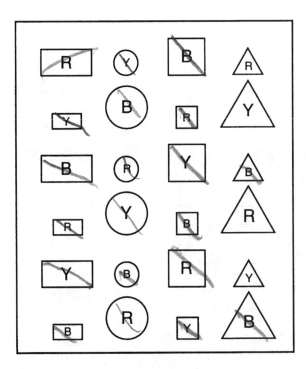

Does It Swim or Fly?

DIRECTIONS: Sort the list of words according to animals that fly and animals that swim.

bass, bat, dolphin, duck, eagle, gull, goose, pike, porpoise, raven, seal, shark, swan, walrus, whale	
FLYERS	**SWIMMERS**

Tumbling Figures

DIRECTIONS: As a shape tumbles along, the side that is on the ground changes. Darken the final two figures to show how they look as they tumble across the page.

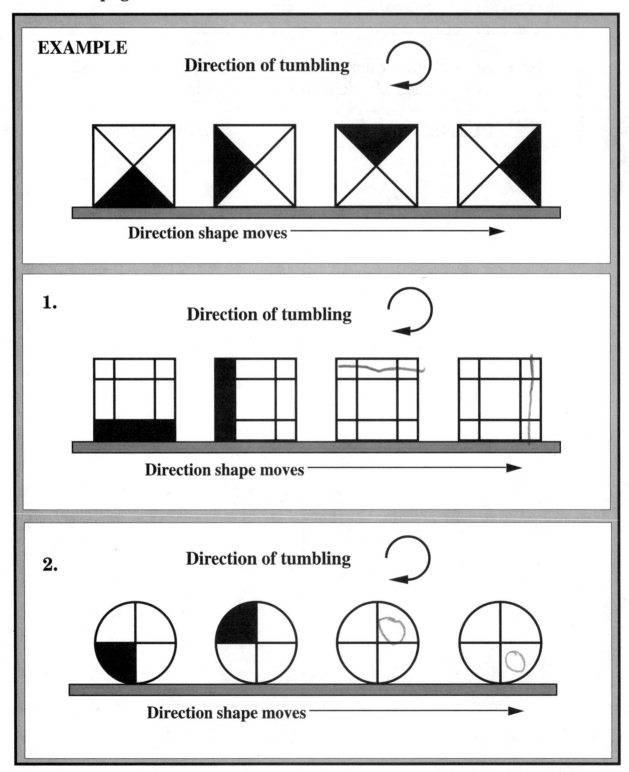

What's Your Guess?

DIRECTIONS: Solve the following number problems and explain your answers.

1. I am a 2-digit number less than 84. The sum of my digits is 9.
    The ones digit is twice the tens digit. Who am I? _____

    Explain how you got your answer.

    _____

    _____

    _____

2. Which would be heavier—a pound of bricks or a pound of paper clips?

Let's Do Riddles

DIRECTIONS: Each line, or pair of lines, in the riddles below contains a clue to the riddle answer. Carefully read each line and try to figure out what is being described. Look for clue words. Try to form a picture in your mind as you connect all the clues. Ask yourself questions about each of the clues. Say or write the answer.

1.

A color like purple,
And I start with V;
I am very pretty,
And I end with T.

What am I? _____

2.

I have two wheels,
And I start with B;
Unless I'm training,
Then see four on me.

What am I? _____

3.

I start and end with S,
And your feet I hide;
Rub me on the mat,
If you've been outside.

What am I? _____

From *Dr. DooRiddles Book A1.* For more activities like the ones above, call 800-458-4849 for the store nearest you or to order directly. © 2002 Critical Thinking Books & Software • www.criticalthinking.com

Those Coins Add Up

DIRECTIONS: You have four coins—two pennies and two nickels. What are the prices of different things you could buy using either two coins or three coins?

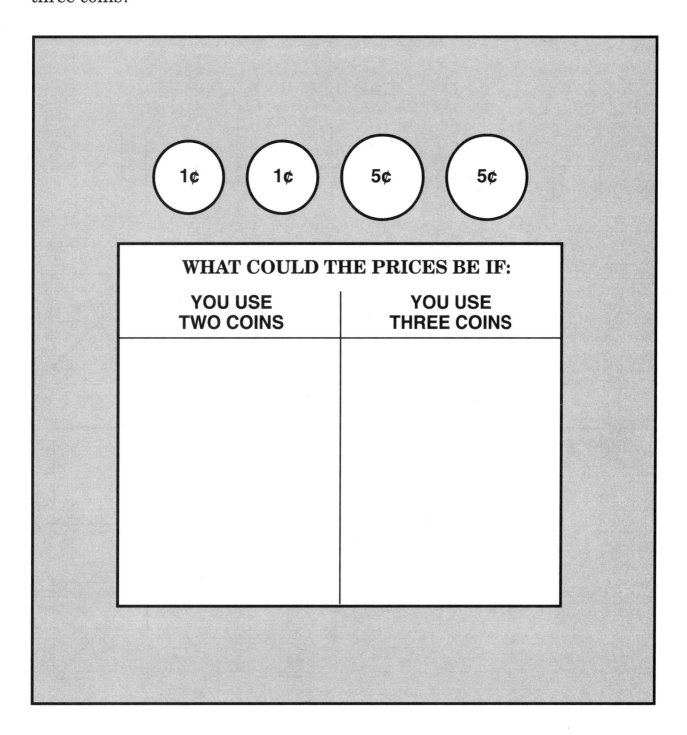

Pattern Search

DIRECTIONS: Circle any figure that contains the letter on the left. Remember, there may be extra lines. The letter must be the same size as the one on the left. Trace over the letter to make sure you are right.

1.

a.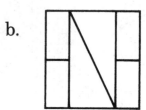

b.

c.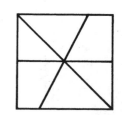

d.

2.

a.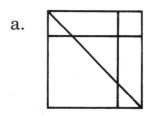

b.

c.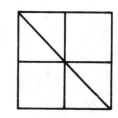

d.

What Do They Have in Common?

DIRECTIONS: Each line contains four words. Read all four words. They all have something in common. Decide what this common thing is, and write it on the line.

> **EXAMPLE** —— **Problem:** ball, wheel, plate, coin
> **Answer:** <u>They all have a round shape.</u>

1. sock, shirt, shoe, jacket

   _____

2. bark, growl, whine, howl

   _____

3. meow, purr, hiss, yowl

   _____

4. sock, shoe, hose, slipper

   _____

5. diaper, bib, booties, bonnet

   _____

6. ice, steam, snow, rain

   _____

7. run, sprint, dash, gallop

   _____

8. braid, curl, bangs, ponytail

   _____

9. elbow, nudge, shove, push

   _____

10. four-leaf clover, rabbit's foot, horseshoe, lucky penny

   _____

From *Basic Thinking Skills: Antonyms, Synonyms, Similarities and Differences.* For more activities like the ones above, call 800-458-4849 for the store nearest you or to order directly. © 2002 Critical Thinking Books & Software · www.criticalthinking.com

Think Literally!

DIRECTIONS: Each of these verbal puzzles is really a common phrase.
Write the phrase in the blanks below.

EXAMPLE: STAND ME   means **Stand By Me**
since **Stand** is next to (by) **Me**.

1.

PEACE
EARTH

_____   _____   _____

2.

_____   _____   _____

Chores in Order

DIRECTIONS: Number the following in the correct order.

1. _____ Take a shopping cart

   _____ Prepare a shopping list

   _____ Pay the cashier

   _____ Leave your house

   _____ Leave the store

   _____ Go to the store

   _____ Put all items in a shopping cart

2. _____ Soap dog

   _____ Fill the tub with water

   _____ Decide it's time to wash your dog

   _____ Dry the dog

   _____ Rinse the dog

   _____ Get the dog wet

   _____ Catch the dog for its bath

Matching Figures

DIRECTIONS: Match the figure in the top row to one of the figures in the bottom row.

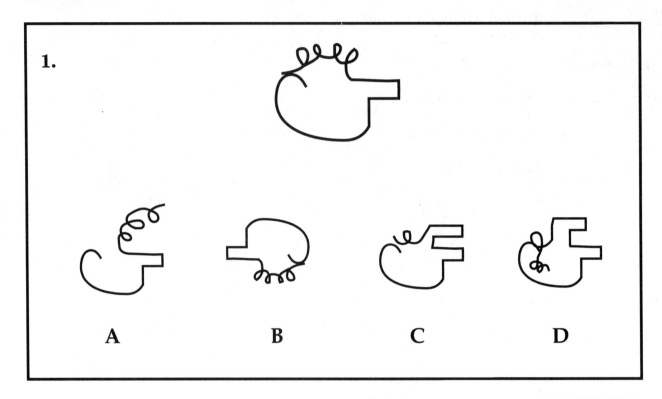

1.

A   B   C   D

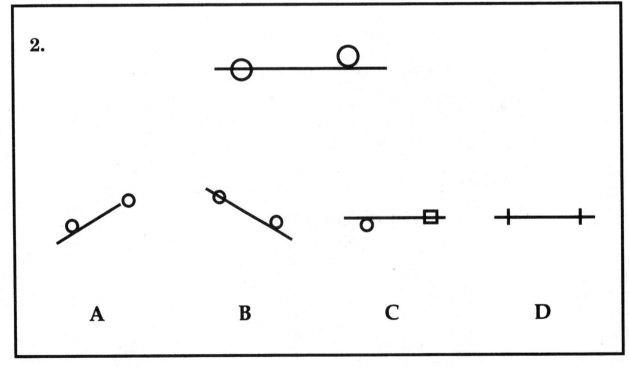

2.

A   B   C   D

Brain Tanglers

1. Five years ago, Samantha was nine years old. How old is she now?

2. Brad's hair is longer than Marlene's. Drew's hair is shorter than Marlene's.

   a. Who has the shortest hair? _____

   b. Who has the longest hair? _____

Pool of Shapes

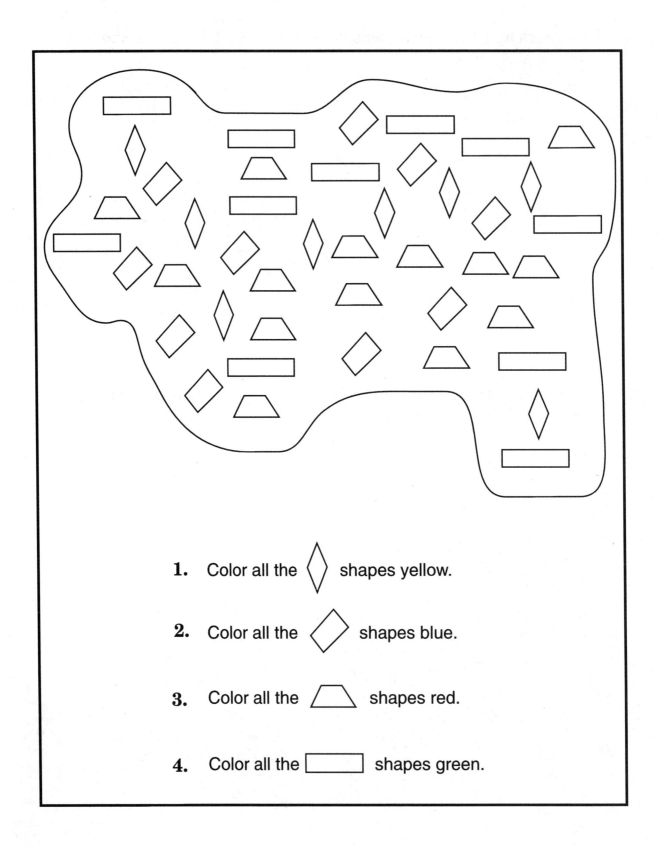

1. Color all the ◇ shapes yellow.

2. Color all the ◇ shapes blue.

3. Color all the △ shapes red.

4. Color all the ▭ shapes green.

18

Four Trios

DIRECTIONS: List the items that come in groups of three.

1. Name the three colors of a traffic light.

_____

_____

_____

2. Name the three bears who met Goldilocks.

_____

_____

_____

3. What did the three little pigs use to build their houses?

_____

_____

_____

4. Name the three daily meals.

_____

_____

_____

Word Matrix

DIRECTIONS: Fill in the boxes of each column with words belonging to that group. Words in each row must all begin with the same letter. Some of the boxes are filled in to help you get started.

FIRST LETTER	PERSON	ANIMAL	VEHICLE
A		Aardvark	
B			
C	Clown		
T			
W			Wagon

Follow the Arrows

DIRECTIONS: Draw the figures as instructed. Then write the word that correctly completes the sentences in the instructions.

1.

a.   Draw a square to the right of the arrow.

b.   Draw a circle in the lower right hand corner.

c.   The circle is _____ the square.

d.   The arrow is to the _____ of the square.

e.   The _____ is in the center.

2.

a.   Draw a circle above the arrow.

b.   Draw a square to the left of the arrow.

c.   Draw a triangle in the upper left corner.

d.   The triangle is _____ the square.

e.   The circle is to the _____ of the triangle.

Yesterday, Today, or Tomorrow

DIRECTIONS: Answer each question with a day of the week.

1. What day is it today, if yesterday was Monday?

    _____

2. If today is Thursday, what day will it be tomorrow?

    _____

3. What day is it today, if yesterday was Saturday?

    _____

4. If today is Tuesday, what day will be tomorrow?

    _____

5. What day is it today, if tomorrow is Sunday?

    _____

6. If today is Monday, what day was yesterday?

    _____

7. What day is it today, if yesterday was Friday?

    _____

22

Copy Cats

DIRECTIONS: Copy the figure shown on the left onto the grid on the right.

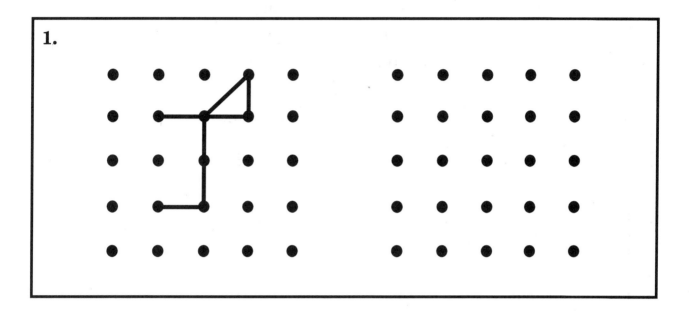

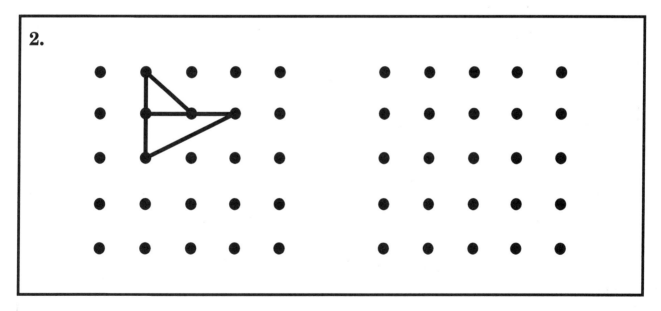

Classifying Shapes

DIRECTIONS: Copy this page. Cut apart the shapes below. For each shape, count the number of sides. Decide whether it is a triangle, quadrilateral, or a pentagon. Classify each shape by the number of sides it has. Place the shapes in the branching diagram on the next page.

Triangles have three sides.
Quadrilaterals have four sides.
Pentagons have five sides.

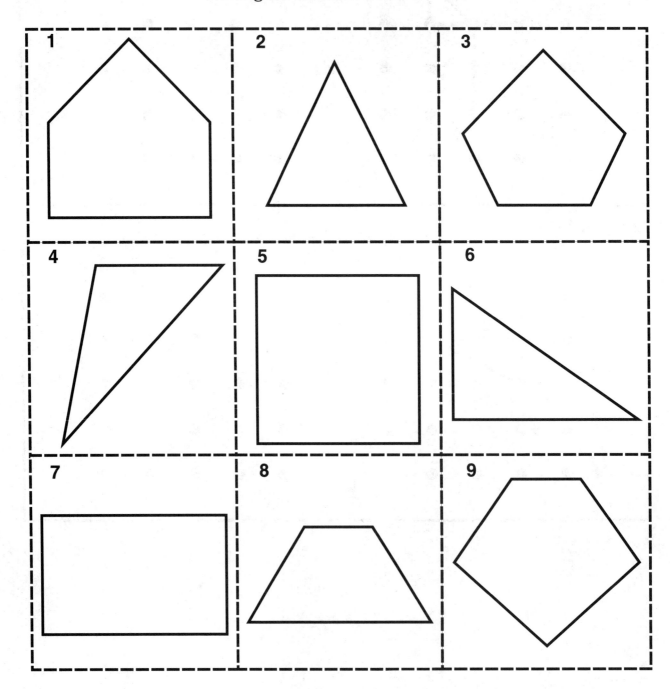

Classifying Shapes

DIRECTIONS: Use the branching diagram below to classify the shapes you cut out from the previous page.

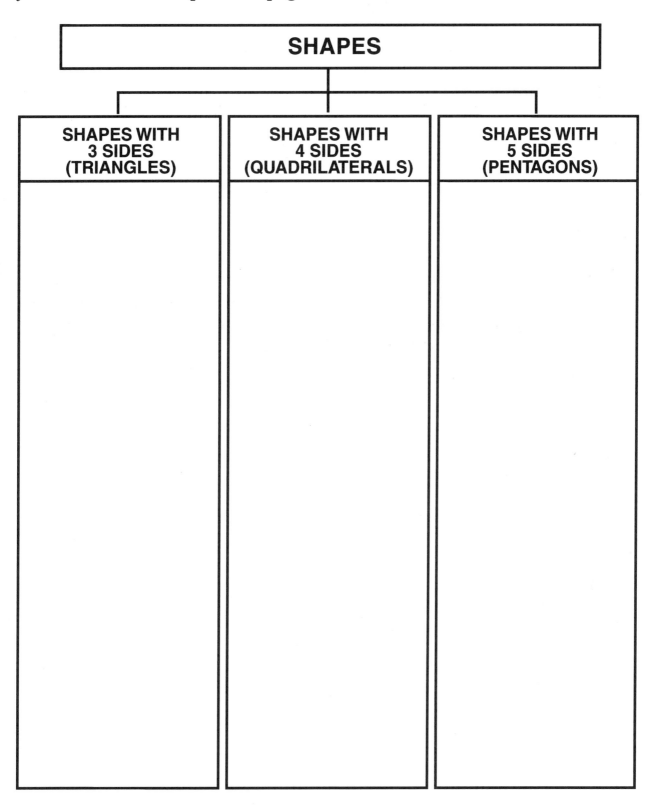

What Do You Think?

1. A maple tree dropped seed pods on the ground. When one of these seed pods starts growing, what kind of tree will it be?

    _____

    How come?

2. Drew looks outside one morning. The sun is shining and there is snow on the ground. There was no snow on the ground when he went to bed last night. He wonders whether it is warm or cold outside. What should he think about the temperature?

3. Andy's kitten likes to chase string. Andy trails a piece of string across the floor in front of his kitten. What will probably happen?

From *Inductive Thinking Skills: Cause and Effect.* For more activities like the ones above, call 800-458-4849 for the store nearest you or to order directly. © 2002 Critical Thinking Books & Software • www.criticalthinking.com

Ranking by Size

A. Number the following from smallest to largest.

_____   sea

_____   pond

_____   ocean

_____   drop

_____   lake

_____   puddle

B. Number the following from largest to smallest.

_____   cantaloupe

_____   grapefruit

_____   orange

_____   peanut

_____   watermelon

_____   plum

From *Language Smarts Book A1.* For more activities like the ones above, call 800-458-4849 for the store nearest you or to order directly. © 2002 Critical Thinking Books & Software • www.criticalthinking.com

Trains

DIRECTIONS: Draw and color or write in the color for the missing pattern blocks in each train.

B = Blue   R = Red   Y = Yellow

Add three more cars to the train, following the same pattern.

1.  B ⃝ B□ B△ B△ B▭ B▭ B□ B□ Y⃝ ___ ___ ___

2. R▭ Y▭ B▭ R▭ Y▭ B▭ R△ Y△ ___ ___ ___

3. Y△ Y▭ Y⃝ Y□ Y△ Y□ Y⃝ Y▭ B△ B▭ ___ ___ ___

Fill in the blank spaces of the train, following the same pattern.

4.  B□ B□ R□ R□ ___ Y□ B⃝ ___ R⃝ R⃝ Y⃝ Y⃝ ___ B△ R△ R△

The Puzzling Truth

DIRECTIONS: Read the following problem. Assume that what is stated in the problem is true. Answer the question listed below.

PROBLEM
If figure 1 is not a cobra, then figure 2 is a hang glider.

1.

2.

QUESTION
Can figure 2 be a bicycle? Circle the correct answer.

Yes

No

More information is needed.

Mystery Letters

DIRECTIONS: Complete the following groups of phrases. Copy the word on the lines below and change the letter in the circle to make a new word.

1.

SAIL   B O A T

RAIN   ◯ __ __ __

CHAR   __ __ __ ◯

FIELD   ◯ __ __ __

MOUNTAIN   __ __ __ ◯

2.

S A I L   BOAT

◯ __ __ __   A LETTER

HOUSE   __ __ __ ◯

◯ __ __ __   AN EGG

◯ __ __ __   THE BILL

SEVERE   __ __ __ ◯

Three Little Kittens

DIRECTIONS: Read the story, then use the chart at the bottom to help you answer the question. Put an X in the box where each kitten did not put its string. The blank spaces will then tell you where each kitten hid its piece of string.

Three kittens were each playing with a piece of colored string. One piece of string was red, one was blue, and one was yellow. When the kittens were called to the kitchen to eat, they each hid their string before going.

One piece of string was hidden under the sofa. One piece of string was hidden behind the TV. One piece of string was hidden under a chair cushion.

When they went back to the living room after eating, they couldn't remember where they had hidden their pieces of string.

"I know I didn't put mine near the sofa," said the kitten whose string was red.

"I didn't put mine by the TV," said the kitten who had been playing with the yellow string.

"I didn't either," said the kitten whose string was red.

Question: Where was each piece of string hidden?

	RED	BLUE	YELLOW
SOFA			
TV			
CHAIR CUSHION			

Figure the Pattern

DIRECTIONS: Use the grid of dots to draw in the shapes that continue the pattern.

1.

2.

3.

4.

5.

From original *Building Thinking Skills® Book 1.* For more activities like the one above, call 800-458-4849 for the store nearest you or to order directly. © 2002 Critical Thinking Books & Software • www.criticalthinking.com

Missing Vowels

DIRECTIONS: Add vowels to the following letters so they correctly spell the name of an animal. For example, D G spells DOG when the vowel O is added. The vowels can be added to the beginning, middle, or end.

P G   _____   F S H   _____

C W   _____   B T   _____

G T   _____   S N K   _____

N T   _____   W L   _____

B   _____   F X   _____

DR   _____   B R   _____

H R S   _____   F R G   _____

W R M   _____   C R B   _____

C T   _____   F L   _____

M S   _____   G S   _____

Paths

DIRECTIONS: How many ways are there to get from A to B? You must follow the lines. You can retrace part of a path to make a new path

1. _____

2. _____

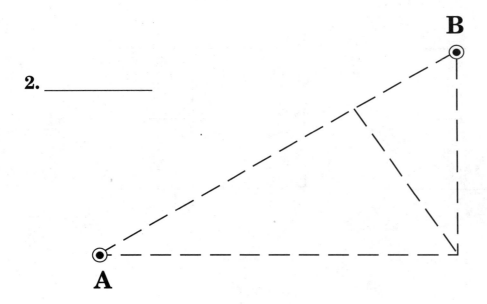

Let's Do Riddles

DIRECTIONS: Each line, or pair of lines, in the riddles below contains a clue to the riddle answer. Carefully read each line and try to figure out what is being described. Look for clue words. Try to form a picture in your mind as you connect all the clues. Ask yourself questions about each of the clues. Say or write the answer.

1.

I stick out of your face,
And I end with an E;
but if you have a cold,
You won't smell much with me.

What am I? _____

2.

I love to eat carrots,
And I end with a T;
I'm so soft and fluffy,
You love to cuddle me.

What am I? _____

3.

A fruit of red or green,
and I start with a G;
You'll find me on a vine,
With more bunches like me.

What am I? _____

Classifying Words

DIRECTIONS: Fill each blank with the word from the box that tells how each pair of words is alike.

> bright   dry   fast   green   hard
>
> slick   slow   soft   wet

1. lamp and beacon are _____

2. fish and water are _____

3. grass and leaves are _____

4. jet airplanes and race cars are _____

5. pillows and whipped cream are _____

6. snails and turtles are _____

7. diamonds and steel are _____

8. oil and grease are _____

9. deserts and dust are _____

From *Verbal Classifications Book A1.* For more activities like the one above, call 800-458-4849 for the store nearest you or to order directly. © 2002 Critical Thinking Books & Software • www.criticalthinking.com

Right Reasoning

1. Isabel goes to school every week Monday through Friday. But she doesn't go on Saturday or Sunday. She wants to rename the days of the week so that all the days except one are either Saturday or Sunday. She figures then that she'll have to go to school only one day a week.

   What's wrong with Isabel's reasoning?

2. Camelia is very frightened of thunderstorms. Every time one comes along, she hides under the bed to make it go away. She knows that hiding under the bed works, because sooner or later the thunderstorm goes away every time she does it.

   What is wrong with Camelia's reasoning?

Think Literally!

DIRECTIONS: This verbal puzzle is really a common phrase. Write the phrase in the blanks below.

EXAMPLE: | STAND ME | means **Stand By Me**
since **Stand** is next to (by) **Me**.

_____   _____

Shape Tables

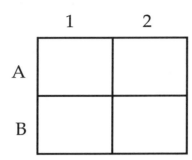

1. Draw a circle in box A1.

2. Draw an X in box B2.

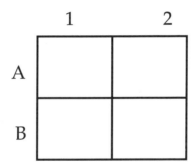

3. Draw a circle in each box of row A.

4. Draw a triangle in each box of row B.

5. Color the circle and triangle in column 1 red.

6. Color the circle and triangle in column 2 blue.

Coin Collection

DIRECTIONS: Solve the money problem using coins or by drawing coins.

Ross has 10 U.S. coins. They add up to 50¢.

What kinds of coins does he have, and how many of each?
     (Hint: There is more than one answer to this problem.)

ANSWER KEY

Page 1: Which Way?

There are 6 ways to get to your friends' house don't forget to count every path—going *with* the arrows only.

Page 2: Pass the Fruit, Please

1. pear, apple, banana
2. lemon, watermelon, grape

Page 3: Number Puzzlers

1. 12. They are both 11 right now (11 + 11 = 22), so next year they will be 12.
2. 25. Subtract the two bottom numbers (smaller from larger) and then double the answer to get the top number.

Page 4: Triangles

15 triangles

Page 5: What is True of Both Words?

1. b. is often round in shape,   d. tells time
2. c. can float
3. b. is in the sky,   c. is round
4. b. can carry one or two people,   c. can move

Page 6: Mystery Blocks

1. small red rectangle
2. large yellow triangle

Page 7: Does It Swim or Fly?

Flyers	Swimmers
bat	bass
duck	dolphin
eagle	pike
gull	porpoise
goose	seal
raven	shark
swan	walrus
	whale

Page 8: Tumbling Figures

1.

2.

Page 9: What's Your Guess?

1. 36. Since you have a 2-digit number, and one digit is twice the other, the smaller digit must be 1, 2, 3, or 4 so the possible beginning answers are 12, 24, 36, 48, 21, 42, 63, and 84. Since the number is less than 84, the answer cannot be 84. That leaves candidates of 12, 24, 36, 48, 21, 42, and 63. Since the ones digit is twice the tens digit, you have 12, 24, and 36. Since the sum of the digits in the answer is 9, the answer must be 36.
2. They both weigh the same—one pound.

Page 10: Let's Do Riddles

1. violet
2. bicycle
3. shoes

Page 11: Those Coins Add Up

You use two coins: 2¢, 6¢, 10¢
You use three coins: 7¢, 11¢

Page 12: Pattern Search

1. a and c
2. b and c

Page 13: What Do They Have in Common?

1. clothes
2. sounds made by a dog
3. sounds made by a cat
4. covers the foot
5. worn by a baby
6. forms of water
7. ways to move fast
8. ways to wear hair
9. ways of moving other people out of the way
10. good luck charms

Page 14: Think Literally!

1. peace on Earth
2. star spangled banner

Page 15: Chores in Order

1. 4
    1
    6
    2
    7
    3
    5

2. 5
    2
    1
    7
    6
    4
    3

Page 16: Matching Figures

1. B
2. B

Page 17: Brain Tanglers

1. 14 years old
2. a. Drew   b. Brad

Page 18: Pool of Shapes

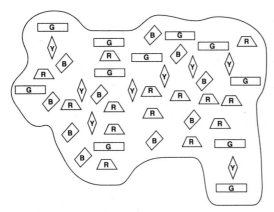

Page 19: Four Trios

1. red, yellow, green
2. Mama, Papa, Baby
3. straw, sticks, bricks
4. breakfast, lunch, dinner (or supper)
   or breakfast, dinner, supper

Page 20: Word Matrix

FIRST LETTER	PERSON	ANIMAL	VEHICLE
A	Aunt	Aardvark	Ambulance
B	Brother	Bear	Bus
C	Clown	Cat	Car
T	Teacher	Tiger	Truck
W	Woman	Wolf	Wagon

*Many answers are possible.

Page 21: Follow the Arrows

1.a. & 1.b.

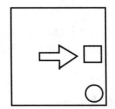

1.c. below
1.d. left
1.e. arrow
2.a.—2.c.

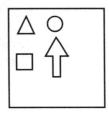

2.d. above
2.e. right

Page 22: Yesterday, Today, or Tomorrow

1. Tuesday
2. Friday
3. Sunday
4. Wednesday
5. Saturday
6. Sunday
7. Saturday

Page 23: Copy Cats

1.

2.

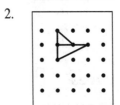

Page 24 & 25: Classifying Shapes

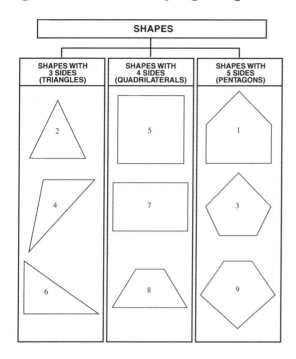

Page 26: What Do You Think?

1. A maple tree. That's the only kind of tree that will grow from a maple tree seed pod.
2. It is cold outside.
3. The kitten will probably chase the string.

Page 27: Ranking by Size

A. 1. drop 2. puddle 3. pond 4. lake 5. sea 6. ocean
B. 1. watermelon 2. cantaloupe 3. grapefruit 4. orange 5. plum 6. peanut

Page 28: Trains

1.
2.
3.
4.

Page 29: The Puzzling Truth

No. Figure 1 is not a cobra, therefore Figure 2 can be only a hang glider.

Page 30: Mystery Letters

1.   SAILBOAT
             RAINCOAT
             CHARCOAL
          FIELD GOAL
      MOUNTAIN GOAT

2.   SAILBOAT
           MAIL A LETTER
        HOUSEMAID
             LAID AN EGG
             PAID THE BILL
      SEVERE PAIN

Page 31: Three Little Kittens

The red string was not near the sofa or the TV (both given), so it was under a chair cushion. Then the yellow string was not under a chair cushion, nor was it behind the TV (given), so it was under the sofa. This leaves the blue string to be behind the TV.

Page 32: Figure the Pattern

repeating group of shapes:

Page 33: Missing Vowels

pig, cow, goat, ant, bee (or boa), deer, horse, worm, cat (or coot), moose (or mouse)

fish, bat, snake, owl, fox, bear (or boar), frog, crab, fly (or flea or foal), goose

Page 34: Paths

1. 3 ways

2. 4 ways

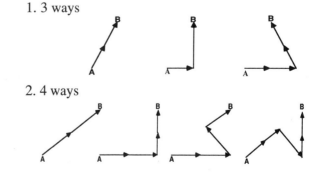

Page 35: Let's Do Riddles

1. nose
2. rabbit
3. grape

Page 36: Classifying Words

1. bright	4. fast	7. hard
2. wet	5. soft	8. slick
3. green	6. slow	9. dry

Page 37: Right Reasoning

1. Isabel thinks the reason she doesn't go to school two days of the week is because those days are called Saturday and Sunday.

2. Camelia thinks she has control over the thunder storms.

Page 38: Think Literally!

horsing around

Page 39: Shape Tables

1–2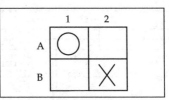

3–6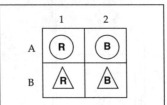

Page 40: Coin Collection

Ross has 10 nickels, or he has 5 pennies, 4 nickels, and 1 quarter.

ACTIVITY/PRODUCT REFERENCE

PAGE NUMBER	ACTIVITY TITLE	SERIES TITLE	OTHER ACTIVITIES FROM THE SERIES
1	Which Way?	Math Ties	
2	Pass the Fruit, Please	Mind Benders®	p. 17
3	Number Puzzlers	Quick Thinks Math	
4	Triangles	Basic Thinking Skills	pp. 13, 36
5	What is True of Both Words?	Building Thinking Skills®	pp. 8, 12, 32, 34
6	Mystery Blocks	Critical and Creative Thinking with Attribute Blocks	p. 28
7	Does It Swim or Fly?	Verbal Classifications	p. 20, 36
8	Tumbling Figures	Building Thinking Skills®	pp. 5, 12, 32, 34
9	What's Your Guess?	Scratch Your Brain	
10	Let's Do Riddles	Dr. DooRiddles	p. 35
11	Those Coins Add Up	Organizing Thinking	pp. 24–25
12	Pattern Search	Building Thinking Skills®	pp. 5, 8, 32, 34
13	What Do They Have in Common?	Basic Thinking Skills	pp. 4, 36
14	Think Literally!	Think-A-Grams	p. 38
15	Chores in Order	Thinking About Time	p. 22
16	Matching Figures	Visual Perceptual Skill Building	pp. 18, 23, 39
17	Brain Tanglers	Mind Benders®	p. 2
18	Pool of Shapes	Visual Perceptual Skill Building	pp. 16, 23, 39
19	Four Trios	Language Smarts	pp. 27, 33
20	Word Matrix	Verbal Classifications	p. 7, 36
21	Follow the Arrows	Thinking Directionally	
22	Yesterday, Today, or Tomorrow	Thinking About Time	p. 15
23	Copy Cats	Visual Perceptual Skill Building	pp. 16, 18, 39
24–25	Classifying Shapes	Organizing Thinking	p. 11
26	What Do You Think?	Inductive Thinking Skills	p. 37
27	Ranking by Size	Language Smarts	pp. 19, 33
28	Trains	Critical and Creative Thinking with Attribute Blocks	p. 6
29	The Puzzling Truth	Beginning Syllogisms	
30	Mystery Letters	Word Benders	
31	Three Little Kittens	Cranium Crackers	p. 40
32	Figure the Pattern	Building Thinking Skills®	pp. 5, 8, 12, 34
33	Missing Vowels	Language Smarts	pp. 19, 27
34	Paths	Building Thinking Skills®	pp. 5, 8, 12, 32
35	Let's Do Riddles	Dr. DooRiddles	p. 10
36	Classifying Words	Verbal Classifications	pp. 7, 20
37	Right Reasoning	Inductive Thinking Skills	p. 26
38	Think Literally!	Think-A-Grams	p. 14
39	Shape Tables	Visual Perceptual Skill Building	pp. 16, 18, 23
40	Coin Collection	Cranium Crackers	p. 3